Birds Of A Feather

**Andrew L. Bouwhuis Library
Canisius College**

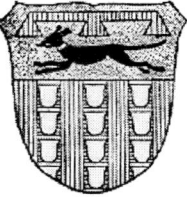

Donated By:

Carl Dennis

Birds Of A Feather

The Complete Poems of Ed Lahey

CLARK CITY PRESS

Copyright © 2005 by Ed Lahey
Printed in the United States of America
All rights reserved.

No part of this book may be reproduced in any manner without the express written consent of the publisher, except in the case of brief excerpts in critical reviews and articles.

All inquiries should be addressed to:
Clark City Press
Post Office Box 1358
Livingston, Montana 59047
(406)222-7412

Book design and author photographs
by Russell Chatham.

Production by Sally Epps, with technical assistance from Cody Redmon.

Special thanks to Richard S. Wheeler
for his thoughtful advice.

First Edition

Library of Congress Control Number: 2004110929

ISBN: 0-944439-56-X [Cloth]

A NOTE FROM THE PUBLISHER

Ed Lahey was a discovery for me in the same way that a blind pig finds an acorn. Idly thumbing through the pages of a *Big Sky Journal*, I came upon an article describing him and his work, and after reading it, felt like I'd slept through an important lecture somewhere in the dim past. It seemed everyone I knew was not only aware of the man, but stood in deep admiration, making me feel like some throwback bumpkin who'd never heard of wine.

Shortly thereafter, while staying in Butte at one of the old three story Victorian houses built around the turn of the century, I found a book of his in one of the bookstores. It was a simple, unpretentious little volume called *The Blind Horses*, which had been put together by the Bookstore at the University of Montana.

The next morning, I awoke as it was getting light, picked up the book, and went downstairs to read in the living room, knowing it could be an hour or more before anyone else in the house would be up. As the sun came slanting through the tall windows, I began to have the feeling I was being hugged overly hard by a giantess, trapped between hard bone and soft bosom. The surprise was completely unexpected, and proved to be inescapable, as the energy flowing from those pages was a force to be reckoned with. I had not been so deeply affected by the written word in a long time.

At this point, before someone decides to launch an investigation into the matter, I hastily admit to not having any proper credentials to criticize or evaluate poetry the way another poet, scholar, or teacher might. I do, however, possess a cultivated aptitude for recognizing art which comes entirely from within, utterly free of motive. Because of this, I can confidently assert that Lahey's work is art at its best; clear, unafraid, humble, sensitive, and straight from a passionate heart.

Writing about earlier collections, Lahey's friend, Buddhist scholar Paul Warwick, had these things to say. "Ed Lahey is tied to Butte, Montana, in dark and passionate ways, and he does not stay away from it for very long. When I say Butte, I mean to include the villages, shacks, and mines in the country around Butte, and the family clan in Corbin in the mountains west of Helena where he still lives part of the time, and, of course, I include the mines which tunnel underneath Butte. Lahey doesn't use images of Butte for external purposes like building a reputation for insight into the workings of the soul; nor does he draw pictures for tourists. He writes for Butte, to Butte, passionate poems, as a son and as a lover. This Butte is not strictly the Butte of today; older times show through. And it is not precisely the Butte of old either. Stories come down filtered through years of whiskey and the tongues of old world languages, the broken English of the country, and there is no particular respect for truth. Even what Lahey sees comes selected. The Butte you enter in his poetry is dark, violent, capricious, sexual, and as highly colored as the Arabian Nights."

And: "He is drawn to elegy. Anger, fear, love and the sadness of loss. Death comes sudden or slow for the people of Butte—Irish miners, whores, ghosts of exiled Confederate soldiers, a boy fallen down an abandoned shaft, old men dying like the old man in *The Blind Horses* still brim full of life. Much of his poetry bears the elegiac tension between a desire to preserve and a certainty of irrevocable loss. Lahey faces the old problems that make poetry universal. He searches down repeatedly in order to return with something poetically true, with metaphors to give shape to troubled emotion, a tale, a gift for a woman, and with luck, a jingle in his pocket."

There are no casual readers of poetry, and that's pretty much a death and taxes fact. Poetry at its best is lyrical, ephemeral, musical, passionate, and often seemingly unusual and obscure to a person accustomed to novels cleverly designed to produce the page turning motion. Accessibility in the arts, which panders to the basest tastes, is most assuredly a negative thing. However, great art, while it has many other complex facets, is always accessible. And Ed Lahey's poems are that, yet they run in deep veins through time, history, and the depth of human emotion, in ways not always obvious.

In commenting on Ed Lahey's poems, one runs out of

superlatives rather quickly. He is everything an artist should be, humble, yet not self-effacing, dignified yet never aloof, confident yet without swagger, strong, yet with never a hint of bullying, emotional, yet never sentimental, sensitive, yet never personally so, melancholy, yet without suicidal tendencies, and naturally, completely soulful.

In an era where the trendy, shallow, and insincere routinely command the stage, Lahey's voice booms a demand for history, depth, and compassion without compromise. He admits his fears, hopes, and frailties readily, in a clear plea for peace and justice. His is poetry purely from the heart, and every author who has ever read his work, has been quick to echo that sentiment. A lion in captivity may still be a lion genetically, although in reality it is altogether diminished. Ed Lahey remains at large, and most certainly will for the duration.

Russell Chatham
Livingston, Montana

Contents

THE BLIND HORSES

THE ORPHAN GIRL PROSPECT	1
THE CLOUD CHASER	2
THE FELL OF DARK	4
TOUGH LAUGHTER	5
THE DUST ON THE FEATHER	6
DIALOGUE OF POET AND PAINTER	7
STONE BEFORE THE CRUMPLED HORN	8
MUCKER'S LAMENT	10
THE BLIND HORSES	12
THE WOUND IN THE HEEL	13
A DIFFERENT PRICE	14
CONTRACT MINERS	15
A LETTER TO THE EDITOR	17
IN MY THREE ACT DREAM	19

THE BALLAD OF THE BOARD OF TRADE BAR	21
LETTER TO THE OWNER OF A GHOST	23
CONFEDERATE SHACKS	25
WINTER NIGHT'S DREAM	27
KELLEY SHAFT CEREMONY	28
THE INQUEST	30
GIMP O'LEARY'S IRON WORKS	32
ICARUS PLANS TO LAND TONIGHT	34
LYRIC FOR O'LEARY	35
ELEGY IN A MINE YARD	36
THE RETURN OF ODYSSEUS	39
EAST OF THE GARDEN CITY	40
POETE MAUDIT	42
QUIESCENT WINGS	43
A GREEN BOX KITE	45
CONTRIBUTOR'S NOTE	46

APPLES ROLLING ON THE LAWN

APPLES ROLLING ON THE LAWN 51

ESSAY POEM #1 53

ROOM FORTY-NINE, FOX HOTEL 54

GRACE 56

THE LONE OUZEL 57

LA PESH 58

THE BEAUTY AND THE BEAST 60

THE MANE OF THE COLD PONY 62

QUICK SILVER RAIN 64

BUTTE, NOUVEAU 65

SWEET TOMATOES 66

MEMOIR 67

BRING ME A COMB FOR MY HAIR 68

OLDE BUTTE RAT 70

CHILD'S PLAY 72

MIDNIGHT BLUE DONKEYS 74

RED TONGUE	75
CHEW ON, CHEW ON	76
WIND HORSE RISING	78
POTATO	80
BLACK CHERRY SPRITZERS	82
ALL MY CHANGE	84

DEEP BELLS

THE OLD POET	89
DR. BUTTE	90
PORTRAIT OF A PHOTOGRAPHER	92
DEEP BELLS	93
THE GREEN LEGEND	95
THE RED CANYON SUITE	97
A WREN'S NEST	99
DREAM INTERROGATIVE	101
FIFTH CENTURY BUTTE	102

A TIP OF THE HAT 103

DUST JACKET 105

NEW POEMS

WINTER RUNOFF 111

SACAJAWEA 112

MINEYARD BLUES 114

THE HOUSE WRECKER 116

THE UPPER BUNK 118

MAIN STREET TABLE CLOTH 119

THE OLD JAZZ POET 121

THE ESCAPE 123

CALL FOR A CAB 125

THE WEB AND STAR 126

JOKERS WILD 127

SMALL SACRIFICE 128

COOL AS A NINE MILE WOLF 129

A CUT OF LIGHT	131
OPEN SPACES	132
CALL TO ARMS	133
GRANDMOTHER	134
APGAR AND AFTER	135
AFTER THE COPPER MINES FAILED	137
LEAVING THE POOL	140
A BLUE SAUCER	141
KATE AND I	142
GRANDDAUGHTER COUNTRY	144
BIRDS OF A FEATHER	145
A NOTE FROM THE THIRD WORLD	147
RACK 'EM UP	148
NO PICK OR SHOVEL	150
FOLK TALE	152
THE CABIN	154
INSIDE HER	155

ROAD KILL	156
A SLICE OF WATERMELON	157
PAPER LANTERNS	159
A WALK WITH ROBERT BLY	160
LOVE ADMITTED, SLEEP DESCENDED	162
HOT SPRINGS	164
LEAVING TOWN	165
SPARROW MEDITATION	167
FORLORN ALLEY	168
WAR GRAY ABSENCE OF SKY	170
STEEL BRACELETS	171
ALDEN NOWLAN MY FRIEND	173
THE MAN NEXT DOOR	175
THE LONG DARK YARD	176
INSIDE THE VIRGIN'S HEAD	178
CARDBOARD SUITCASE	180

for Marylor Wilson

THE BLIND HORSES

THE ORPHAN GIRL PROSPECT

Deep in mined-out waste
carbide lamps illuminate mold,
black damp in a caved-in raise.
Shattered quartzite seams
crack inside the mountain
where quick men move
(in calculated haste)
to fill pant-leg sample sacks
with gob and crumb.

Ore sleeps in blankets,
copper, gold, or silver lace.
Visions in spring dreams
drift like smoke from shacks
where women read catalogues
and put up fruit—in case.

The heavy snow comes quick as rage
some men whose wives grow grim
as quartz, or jasper stone,
leave the worked-out stopes,
trudge back to safer jobs,
collect a union wage.

On the rim
between the mountain
and their hopes,
other fools, maybe wise,
laugh and wait.

THE CLOUD-CHASER

On the rib of a hill
not far from arid farms
the ragged cloud-chaser waits,
twirling his bone whistle
in tune with the wind
like a twister's hum.

The dance begins:
A white cloud forms from the drift
of a skyblue day.
A watery eye glides over the ground,
blind as the cactus sponge
the cloud-chaser hugs in his arms.

The ragged man waves at the sky,
tests the earth with his tongue,
prepares for his race
with the rolling stone of the sun,
dances on each grain of sand
as he follows the cloud.

The men of the village gather
fearing disaster and thirst.
They chatter about the cloud-chaser
who may be confused by the orange
of the moon. He may be insane:
They are sad without rain.

The villagers mutter,
    "The chaser of clouds is back.
    He carries the sky on his shoulder.
    He comes empty handed,
    no scripture, no tablets in stone."

Sane women circle him tossing their hair
singing and joyous with laughter,
holding him close in their eyes
lightly kissing his skin
for a taste of the rain.

THE FELL OF DARK

He stood on the ice-hard road
in his long johns,
white against the muddied snow,
his rear end blue
in the whipping wind,
bare as a soul,
his fist clenched in a curse of rock.

Crystals shagged his hair
as he cursed the mountain down,
honest as steady snow
drifting past the window.
"Fuck you," he shouted,
and the wind hurled his words
to the ground.

From the timber of his rage
it came like a stalking horse
out of a dark cloud
to split his uncrowned harp
like an oak mine-wedge
hammered home with a slam
that even the Pope didn't hear.

Left in the cabin alone,
his woman said to the wind,
"He took all of the risks."
And the cold night whispered
and poked at her chimney
with fingers sharp as a thief's.

TOUGH LAUGHTER

She came.
It was dark in the shaft,
the flame from her light
was sheer fire in the pitch-
black drift—moving like a dream.
He thought,
what if I awake?
The nightmare of caved-in timber
broken head boards, a stull,
cracked like a tooth
in a stone fist, 3600 feet
below the surface
and the daylight,
and she came,
arms reaching for him,
gathering him up
with tough laughter
as if to say,
"Now you've gone and done it,
and no damned insurance either."

THE DUST ON THE FEATHER

Birds wheel in dirty light.
Pulleys sag from rusted beams
in this mill my father worked.
Quiet dissolves the wings.

Father Fritz, in his black coat,
never saw a sample sheet,
when he said politely to no
inquiry, "The Church will not,
can not, bury him. I'm sorry."

Crusted with low-grade ore
the old man tried to ship,
the gears won't turn again
a piston in the engine frozen.

The priest had his reasons,
could hardly know how rooky
birds and radar-clicking bats
win reports and roost on hearts.

Crows and starlings have no season
to loot the nests below the roof.
My eyes avoid the swallow
in the silt and feathered dust.

DIALOGUE OF POET AND PAINTER

Undeniably she knew anatomy.
The bone and the form did not trouble
her bright brush line. The flesh
was her problem. Hard like bacon,
or refrigerated lard rubbed over
bones that she knew to the marrow,
the flesh hung there useless.

"Broil off the fat" I said,
sounding heavy myself and aware
of the roll above my belt,
"No" she said, as I undid
her tunic with a smooth zip,
feeling the answer muscle
the flesh like a metaphor.

STONE BEFORE THE CRUMPLED HORN

Indigo's brown eyes blurred, hot
like the hurt eyes of a cornered fox
when McGuire's trombone brogue
shouted war, as he downed the double shot,
cracked a bottle back across the bar
and slammed that brass spittoon to gong
against the smoked-up wall.

Indigo was the darkest Mexican in town,
a stropped razor buckled to his belt.
McGuire knew that night he'd fought
his last good fight fifteen years before
he'd turned stone-slow, stiff by talk
and muscled bluff, refuge of a dying king.

Listening to Indian blood roar
Comanche through his swelling veins
Indigo called him out
to sack him on the sawdust floor,
his blade the end of words,
sharper than dramatic temper,
or any other Irish act.

Silhouettes along the bar watched
until a Spanish girl with no pants
danced like black gunpowder in a dream
to the center of the scene to lift
explosive skirts and pirouette
naked before the tiger's teeth.

The bartender of The East Park Plaza
rolls bone dice with juke box takers
tells the tale with scorn,
saved her pants, a trophy dropped,
does not understand black powder
as did the blasted men—
stone before the crumpled horn.

MUCKER'S LAMENT

In the Belmont shaft
down thirteen levels
Mike Quill's ghost presides.
(Some say he was an Irish Mason.)
The miners refuse
to acknowledge heresy;
they confound devils
by tracing the sign of the cross
before the underground station.

If the Masons don't get you
the barleycorn will. . . .

Last week Mucker Malone
ignored the ritual,
or so the nipper,
One-Eyed Nelson, said.
Nelson, a Cousin-Jack,
doesn't believe
"in all that rot."

If the Masons don't get you
the barleycorn will. . . .

But Blonde Edna,
the Mucker's whore,
dreams him dead
in a copper casket;
and he's hitting the bottle
a lot.

If the Masons don't get you
the barleycorn will. . . .

The shifter doesn't care.
So the Mucker,
he takes the cage,
goes down drunk
thirteen levels
to meet Mike Quill.

If the Masons don't get you
the barleycorn will. . . .

THE BLIND HORSES

The old man in the hospital bed
with his horny yellow foot
stuck through the stainless rails,
claimed that July night—the one he picked to die on—
he smelled sulfur on his gown.

When he was my age he worked the lower levels of the
Lex in a great underground corral, yoked iron tongue to
wagons filled with ruby silver and peacock copper rock,
flaked sweet hay to horses, shot the worn out.

Dozens of tramway horses hauled hard
against whippletrees—rubbed the timbered tunnels
clean—pulling down the cribbed-up drifts,
brass lanterns swinging, work bits in their teeth,
slick with mine damp and cold to the touch.

Dry stulls in the crosscut cave of that stone corral caught
fire in '98. The horses, tunnel-blind from lack of light,
burned up in the green flame that licked the lagging
black in the Lexington Mine.

I met his eyes cracked white
like a drunk's who hasn't had a drink in months.
He said he could hear hoofbeats ring
and click against the granite footwalls.
He complained of being cold. His nostrils flared:
"I hear them breathing, Ed."

THE WOUND IN THE HEEL

It finally makes no difference,
critics who do not love me,
who charge me with their cherished
instruments—certain to cause
lockjaw. I am not going anywhere.

It finally makes no difference
the men are loved for the wrong reasons,
the nail in my heel is more harmful,
harder to ignore than the wound
of a blue pencil.

Critics and women should love me,
I consider them people and treat them
as such, as though they were poems.
It finally makes no difference.
Seasons will see to that.

It finally makes no difference,
the blood in my boots is warm.
Words are not sharp jabs of steel,
not real like a nail,
but I cannot go on saying,

"It makes no difference" even though,
finally, it does not make any difference.

A DIFFERENT PRICE

Topside,
a bull gear caught Haggerty's hand,
slick iron on a wet day.
I heard him speak to it.
"Whoa," he said.
It cut his hand off anyway.

To release the claim
and settle the debt
officials gave Haggerty
a hoister's chair
in the Neversweat.

Last week his ghost hand
missed a grip
dropped six men
a thousand feet.

The Company will pay for that
I understand.

CONTRACT MINERS

Underground we fought the earth together.
For the hell of it, and Peacock copper.
From the womb she was no tender lover.
The stone-boat rocker wouldn't budge
a crumb to a beggar's cup,
or toss a meatless bone
to a blind man's bitch. Until we made her.
Compressor moan and drill chatter
in her lamp-lit face
forced surrender from the stone.

Midwife to the mine he taught me how
to spit a round and slant a lifter.
He grinned greenhorn at my back
when I smelled fear curl thru the drift
and cling to shaky fingers
as each to each they lit spliced fuses
one by one. And then we ran,
down the cross-cut tunnel
Soon the shudder of ground
brought us back to witness birth.

The mice sat in the corner of our eyes.
They were wise. We watched them listen
to the timber groan beneath
gravid loins of working earth.
With care and art, mindful of the mice,
we imitated moles. We spilled thru mealy
low grade zones to court her frigid heart,
where once solutions boiled
and, dying darkly, cooled.

A LETTER TO THE EDITOR

Instead of "I like it"
someone said
the Chamber of Commerce slogan
should have read,
"Butte is my town,
let's face it"
which I couldn't.

Surface wit will not
dampen a ghostly rattle.
The cough of Miner's Con
is heard hacking
silicotic glitter.

How could I,
whose grandfather kissed
with flaky lips
(evidence of ruined lungs)
live with all that wit?

Should I ignore
the brittle whore
whose rotten-flower thighs
smothered old Sean,
while flat-hat Commercemen
chat about litterbugs.

> "Filth in the street,
> debris, garbage cans
> volunteers, radon daughters,"
> the paper said.

I remember Sean
sad out of a rustling card
drunk and puking sharp death.
"They're all skymers, Ed,
every Mother one,
and they hung Mucky Malone
to the Rocker Bridge."

Papers came out as usual,
Father Fritz said the last rites,
and I bled salty love
from the corner of wake eyes
down generous legs
of Sean's little girl.

So suck up your own litter,
file it in your copper shat,
blow it down the Kelley,
belch in a Mexican miner's face
before he tastes
your brand of chili.

IN MY THREE ACT DREAM

I'm underground again
with Crazy Dan the Buzzy wrecker,
hand hooked up to a widow-maker
mind burned out by what I know of men
with many mouths and palms
rubbed slick and thin
by polishing the shifter's boot.
The powder whip, the heave of bleeding
ruby silver from a high grade round
runs red the turnsheet
of another man's cutter.

On a rocking cage and payday's just a shack
at the edge of the great pit's lip
where my green-eyed girl with the apple breasts
shakes out stars like laundered linen
as she walks in her lovely way.
Swag lines my pocket. My belt buckles
at the side of the springing bone,
love's the game, and laughter,
lush as the good corn bourbon
smoking my liver.

Topside and out of cribbing timber
a well-cast drill chuckles like a hammer.
She rubs the ache, and after,
I take the day easy in the lap of the girl
with the white round hips.
Her brown hair braids my waist,
lifts me from the wings of pitch black stopes
up raises of the night and free
of the working earth.
The candle of the smelter stack
laves copper rings around the moon.

THE BALLAD OF THE BOARD OF TRADE BAR

Coal Oil Belle
was a red lamp legend
in a brown town.
She worked her trade
behind a smelter stack
in the echo
of the night shift whistle.

Her polished symbol,
the hurricane lamp,
red as a Black Widow's belly,
swung in bronze relief
—an evening star—
above the dark oak door
of the Board of Trade bar.

Belle's fame is now renowned.
In a town of misery
one needs sentimental history.
I've never heard it said
that anyone thinks it strange
they often neglect to tell
of the Madam's final bed,
a two thousand dollar
engraved coffin.

Lined with silver
beneath a smoking torch
ten pounds of bone.
Her house is in the ground.
Some men know
when the whistles blow
her earless sockets listen,
as her hip bones move
to the pocket sound
of a lover's jingle.

LETTER TO THE OWNER OF A GHOST

I was visiting with your poem
"The Way A Ghost Dissolves"
knowing you might have
written it with a burnt match
on butcher paper or a grocery wrap
if your pencils were lost,
or cut it into a piece of slate
lugged down from the mountain.

Here's news:
Bulldozers have mucked up your house.
The outline of the kitchen stands.
At night walking in the waste
I hear belly laughter defeating
the slice of the cat's blade,
chuckling in the sink drain
where time and so much ice melted.
Some ghosts do not fade.

They live in unoccupied space.
If you cradle an ear and listen
you can hear the fat man talk,
courtly host, unlucky lover,
King of the Khyber Rifles.
Or see the face,
quick image from a lost station
broadcasting from Atlantis.

In a letter a poet shouldn't boast
so come back home from Italy,
and I'll show you what I mean.
Even if they have planted lawn
over the grave of your house
some substantial part will remain
to cheat the grass and iron cat
that tries to doze away your ghost.

CONFEDERATE SHACKS

I snowshoed over windfalls,
and watched hawks circle
Confederate Gulch.
Now gray ghosts inhabit homesteads
and the pain of Southern deserters
dissolves into wood rust
beneath hawk shadow and the ache
of a hundred winters.

Each Northern drift crusts
thicker than Sherman's rubble.
Spirits in battered hats
haze whisker-frozen cattle
into wind-break barns.
They ditched the glory of the myth
and came from Southern hunger
to meet wind and canyon
far from managed battle.

Five miles up the gulch and tired,
the snow-starched shack,
glazed remains of a weathered bunker
far from Shiloh.
Ice jarred the door case
but ricks of wood banked,
not around the walls
to freeze in place.

What storm battalions could not do
I did by lifting up the latch.
Inside gone black in ash
of a decomposing room,
a shattered comb,
a picture of a woman,
yellow from back home,
a letter.

"Dearest…
         Forgive me … Daddy says …"
When I left I slammed the goddamn door.

Hawks in sun sail
echoes over monstrous tracks.
It makes no difference.
No smoke rises from dead shacks.

WINTER NIGHT'S DREAM

I would have you see a sign
so I pen these lines:
A dance against the wind
a line of geese
curving out of kind
turn in feathered flight—
I thought—mirage,
too hard to even steal
and now with you
the night promises something new
the days again are real . . .

KELLEY SHAFT CEREMONY

In New York City
fifty priests say mass
for Cornelius Kelley,
cartel kind of copper.
Ground wind in his copper camp
howls winter requiem in Butte.

Half-mast hoist house flags
whip attention.
Shifters cream lukewarm lies
into bitter coffee cups.
Cold white skin men
dress in Drys and prepare
to descend in silent stream.

Shaft lights flicker, helmets click,
as someone shuffles on the grate.
A lame Finn drops his bucket
crowds a Mick.
Both men mutter in the cage
at a company suck
sent to ritual
at the portal stage.

To honor Kelley
he makes an inscribed
copper plate
fit screw holes
in the gallows frame.
Now men slip down the throat
of a dead man's monument.

THE INQUEST

Gasoline, cracked chrome, twisted spokes,
a mangled Dream rubs its paint
on tangled rock along that country road
where often we raced—
sparrow hawks swooping low
beside fence posts and willows
tracking the black new road,

and now he's dead.

Strange that he would choose
to slip through fog this morning
knowing water on the road
calls for blood. He went alone.
He did not bang upon my door
with his dark Italian helmet,
nor did I hear his decorated laughter.

I cannot explain.

I do not think he wished to die.
He was not a complicated man.
Perhaps something went wrong,
and he could not feel the rain
pooling on the pavement,
rising from the spinning wheel,

and now he's dead.

I heard him kick the engine over
or maybe I dreamed I did.
I tried to warn him, I think,
struggling in my sleep,
trying to compete with the bike's
beginning. "Watch the road," I said,
or thought I did, as he slipped
into the pocked face
of the rain this morning.

And now he's dead,
and I cannot explain.

GIMP O'LEARY'S IRON WORKS
(for Big Ed)

You hear a lot of lies about O'Leary
but he could seal a crack in steel
no matter what the size.
His arc welder would strike
white fire and a bead
of blue-black rod would slide
along between cherry streaks,
and acrid smoke would curl away
to leave clean married steel,
not too frail, or buttered up
but straight and strong,
hard as mill forged rail.

Of course you might say,
"Don't use that example
as a metaphor for poetry.
Welding is a matter of utility."
And you'd be right. Still,
I remember the look on his face
when he'd lift his great helmet
and sneak up on the finished
job with his unprotected eyes.
It was always between him
and the piece of steel—
a struggle of molecules and will.

Often others would say to him,
"Damn good job" or some such thing.
If it was, he'd grin, and look again,
as if he thought the natural light
would show a flaw, or bridge
that didn't fuse—convinced, I guess,
that in his struggle with the steel
he could seldom really win.
He knew perfection could
conceal the wound
beneath the arc of his art.
I liked him for that.

ICARUS PLANS TO LAND TONIGHT

The lights on the earth are villages
or trampled stars burning on the ground
in clusters.

The wind hums in the darkness,
pulling me over familiar country,
over green meadows and forests.

I am expected at a reunion
in a crowded room across the sea
beyond the usual mountains.

Old acquaintances will complain
when I step from my paper plane
that I have changed.

What I will do for the sake of fashion
is simply set fire to my wax wings
then land and blow away the smoke

and carefully brush the ashes
from my legs which I keep for walking
on such occasions.

LYRIC FOR O'LEARY

Out of range of the Minnie Jane fault
past the lope of the big machine
the foot wall floats and head boards moan
"Thirty bucks a day to clear the stope."

What do we care if the hanging wall slips?
What do we care if the timber's green
and the coffin hoist calls from the mouth
of the shaft? We will drink bourbon and cream
and laugh at O'Leary's wake, argue and sing.

We will uncover the mucker's bones,
gather them up for Mary.
And the company will pay us big money.
Goddamn it. Come on. Let's dig up O'Leary.

ELEGY IN A MINE YARD

I passed the gate and skull
that whistles in the wind—
a hide, rag, bone-barrier
that spooks cows and fascinates kids
—and always did—
the cattle guard entrance to the canyon,

called Cataract. The trail is steep.
From the view binoculars provide,
gallus frames collide to shape
designs of pain, and shacks
dissolve in rock and dust

on Taboo Hill where hoist drums
rust and slant toward glory holes
that gape like hungry mouths
of stone giants banged wide
by lust.

Every year from the town below
volunteers came to hammer, nail,
and board, Fathers and brothers
or young men looking for free beer,
plank some shafts with tamarack
timber and curse the ones they can't.

Old men chaw tobacco and swap lies,
and wag their heads and talk
of me and Dave and Connie Joe,
and of the weather in this canyon.
Summer or winter, it damn near
always threatens snow.

They're not there now, but I can
see them just the same.
I remember at the funeral
how they came—wearing stone faces,
true to our kind on such occasions.

Forgotten images return—
the small white coffin,
Dave, standing of all places,
between Mrs. Murphy and a downtown cop,
kicking the freshly turned earth
with a curious polished shoe,

the black Ford cars in solemn rows,
the priest in worn clothes,
who said the requiem and asked for grace,
and coughed when Connie's sister came
to sing a coranach
before the casket and the grave,

the apple trees that moved in wind
to shed moist bells of red upon the lawn.
Those trees we stole from often,
since they grew in sacred ground,
and in a Catholic cemetery
where a bishop disapproved.

Since I've come this far
binoculars and memory will not do.
I'll climb Taboo Hill to see
just where he fell—
walking as he always did,
a skip or two in front of Dave and me.

I'll come down slower
than on that day
we ran a mile for men with rope,
who shook their heads and knew,
there wasn't any hope,
if what we said in terror was true.

They've posted a cross
on the gate before the shaft,
and a sign where my apple stealing friend,
Cornelius Joseph Daly died
in the year of our Lord 1948,
as if to indicate
       the loss
              is covered
              by the date.

THE RETURN OF ODYSSEUS

"Give me the bow. I can still string it.
I'll send an arrow to the center."

He shuffled toward the bedroom hatrack
hung his wilted coat upon a horn
and pulled from his quiver
the straightest arrow he could muster.
Before Penelope could get up
he placed the arrow to the bow.

"Zeus" she exclaimed from her bed,
"The old fool has returned from the front
and would you look at his hands shake
and the veins bulge in his head."

"I have been on a long trip." he said,
"But as you can see the rumor is wrong,
I am not dead. I am only planning my death.
What suitors drink mead from my mug?"

"They are friends who have worried,
come to comfort me in my need.
You've been gone a long time, after all.
Now sheath up your arrow. You must wait.
I have shopping to do and people to call."

And she left him to sleep with the dog
who knew him and liked his smell.

EAST OF THE GARDEN CITY

He crouched on the mirror
of ice inside the drain pipe
by a rack of antlers
pitched from a hunter's kill.

He listened to cars whistle
through space overhead,
seeing bright red turbines
spin like hunting caps in wind.

The static in his brain
blocked further transmission.
He kicked at the elk's horns
on the floor of the tunnel.

The "Best People on Earth."
He remembered the lodge,
jokes about women and meat,
so much a pound.

She was dancing, watching him,
loving him later
in the loft of the barn,
warm and soft in his arms.

He heard someone talking,
dark manifest forces,
patterns of compensation,
saw blood and animal surprise
on the face in the ice,
as he fell toward the horns,
dropping his father's pistol
in the drainage tunnel.

East of our town.

POETE MAUDIT

I see him stagger in the rain
hugging the brown paper sack,
lurching toward the goddess
at the end of his vision.

I am not morally opposed,
nor do I think he's a talent wasted.
He holds the bottle like a gun
loaded with these sentiments.

Shot by shot he pulls the trigger,
quoting Rimbaud as he goes,
willing his failure to die
in an undramatic manner.

QUIESCENT WINGS

Last night, coming in late,
I brushed the lilac tree, casually,
thought no more about it until,
while on the phone to you,
I heard him buzz angrily—
inside my shirt—
I tore off quickly in panic
and had no choice but to stay
with him in the dark room
as he bumbled about buzzing madly
about my head,
sounding like an angry God
about to strike down a sinner.

This morning when I found him dead,
it was a shock he was so small,
his crumpled wings limp against his body
lying there on the floor of the room
he had filled to the brim
with his last buzz.

I confess I half expected to find
his stinger wedged
like a bayonet in something hard
like a sill.

Or maybe when I go to shave
find it protruding from my jaw.
He was after me with every lash
of his now quiescent wings.

A GREEN BOX KITE
(for the S & S girls)

Again wet wind whips the river,
ice boils down the mountain pass,
the earth crumbles in the thaw.
A kite sails into clouds
spilling from my eye.

We have promises to keep,
an Easter egg hunt in the park,
laughter deep within,
songs to sing, minds to bend,
children rolling on the lawn.

Before the swell of summer heat,
before the mowers come,
a great bat will rise into the sky
with phosphorescent eyes,
I will wear my gray felt hat,

watch that great black bat
fly away winter on icy wings,
far back, back into the mind
to circle the word—a green box kite
made of balsa wood,

light enough to catch the eye,
fleet enough to meet the wind,
awkward enough to stand the storm,
big as any ark ever built,
hooked to a lover's string.

CONTRIBUTOR'S NOTE
(for Jim Gilman)

I rode a motor
thru a tramway tunnel
in the Mountain Con,
listened to the brass
bell clang as the skip
hoist banged the bucket
up the number two shaft.

The Kelly men worked
in the open stope,
barred down rock
from a bald head raise
to the gopher crews
who mucked around
the goddamn clock.

They coughed up soot
but silica stuck,
as widow-makers howled
when the Ingersoll moaned
and the starter steel struck
the hornblende stone.

I burned images black
on the hanging wall
with a spitter's lamp,
drank brackish water
from a tin can cup
and grew hands hard
with knotted knuckles.

And I cleaned track
with a moron's claw,
scraped the turnsheet down
with a flat Finn hoe,
bird in an alligator's jaw.

Lost in a drift of teeth
I dreamed a lot.

APPLES ROLLING ON THE LAWN

APPLES ROLLING ON THE LAWN

I am sitting in a trailer
listening to the nerve of a chain saw
cut ten years from the image of a man,
worrying a loose key in my Underwood Jaw,
a tooth that bothers the tongue,
a twitch in my up-to-date clone.

A ripe Macintosh just fell off the roof
from a tree that sheds deliciously,
a pleasing sound, but it bothers me
that I don't know you anymore
dark inside the shut core of that apple
rolling red on ground outside my door.

Remember that decorated ukulele
that fell from the Buckhouse Bridge
we walked together? Or did you
drop it in the river to hear
the splash of baroque art? Or hear
tinsel music disappear forever?

Do you still wear a beard? Or some other
signal of defiance? What can I say
in a letter to someone who is editing
Henry Miller? Your ghost comes from years,
a curious skip of TV from afar,
a sign you aren't lost in space.

Herringbone on the face of the image
makes me fear the picture I seek on paper.
Years harden us like scars. I could phone,
but what if the wires were dead
when I went to call? Or when I reached you
I found myself alone on the line?

What if you said, "Hello," in a voice
I don't know at all? And I could hear
the tree strain in the wind, hear the apple fall
then slowly roll into a ring of moist red bells
to claim the well kept grass,
and that was all?

ESSAY POEM #1

I have pulled my blinds.
All day I have listened to the traffic
beyond my sight. My quarters are cool.
Dirty though. Crusty. Cajun Irish maybe.
Or Butte, American.

The shrubbery in my apartment
is eccentric, a nest of wild plants,
leaves spreading about. A dry bush
that contains a large picture
of an owl, his head turns around
like a Missoulian.

Books piled about strategically,
the guardians of a fragile mind
brought face to face
with impossible thought,
the challenges, the questions.

Nowhere to go exactly but eclectic,
the trippy diversity of now.
Perhaps like the owl I am a caged bird,
in a fantasy having something to do with wisdom?

The dignity of meek nesting with the dignity
of outrageousness. It could be easily
painted as crazy, my quarters, yet
they are warm in the winter,
cool and inscrutable in the summer.

ROOM FORTY-NINE, FOX HOTEL

I will die on somebody's birthday.
It is always that way with us,
striving to become
a minor poet.

Writing a letter to someone
in Canada, may it be you,
probably in February,
warm in my coat, Dr. Zhivago.

A rose from a stranger
I know I could love,
a cup of coffee with ice cream,
a dollop floating,
rich as my life,
North Star French Vanilla
cooling in the mug she threw
by the bed,
an unread letter on pink paper:

"Dear Ed,
You qualify for the job,
our janitor is dead. We know
you could fill his shoes, the work
is not hard. We were impressed
with your experience on the University's
labor maintenance gang.

The Super likes your poetry.
He did not know
what you meant when you wrote
you 'believed in the mysticism of the Union.'
but the job is still open
and pays $180.00 a month.

Gracie said she could get you in, Local 306,
if you get my meaning,
but you must join.
Hope you are feeling better,
nothing worse than a dither."

GRACE

Beside the Clark's Fork River
looking at a Russian Olive tree
just budding at the edge of the water
the crippled black man sat, pointing.

"Look at those buds," he said.
"Bugs!" Sara said, "bugs?"
peering suspiciously at the tree.

We laughed at the significant buzz
that skimmed our thoughts,
the ambiguity of winged things,
the old black guy, my daughter and I,
waited quietly by the stroller
as the river, the old town toilet,
sloshed by, a flush of water,
white over gray rock.

"Buds," I whispered.

THE LONE OUZEL

He is a strange bird,
perched upon one leg,
peering into the stream
that breaks over the rocks,
taking only a thousand years
to polish the troubled stone.

It will be getting dark soon
in this small rented room.
My ghost, the miner with the silky dead hair,
will soon return,
drift in, but say nothing
of the branch I've whittled down,
nor mention the peeled bark,
the nest around my wet shoes.

The dipper is deep in the water,
the ghost will say nothing
of my reflections,
or ask abstruse questions.
The creek is closer when he comes.
Its waters flow past us, older than him,
older than me.

LA PESH

She was curled up
with large furry animals,
floppy eared spaniels!

She thought about the novelist
who said, "You look like a swimmer."
She wondered about words!

Who knew what to say,
or was it "just an old star, anyway?"
Did it really even have a name?

What is that red light
on top of a mountain called Sentinel?

Why does she even look
out her window? Is there a poem
in the garden? Can girls be gifted?

Her hair hung down in ringlets.
She was glad for the dogs around her,
the flame of candlelight.

Someone had taken a little step
for himself, then a big step for mankind,
then jumped around on the face
of the moon in a goofy suit.

She remembered Disneyland.
Thought again about the novelist
and wondered if her name
should have been La Pesh?

Or was it some kind of test?
Would she have to swim the English Channel!
Or could she go on writing poems?

THE BEAUTY AND THE BEAST

I celebrate my fate
claim no union or enterprise,
unless it's with the dead
who never made the grade,
tasted much of money
or of fame, no winning hand
in apex law, glory holes,
or real estate.
Dust to dust. Debts are paid.

I salute the ruins
of the Neversweat
on my hilly morning climb,
take the time to pet
Centerville Sally's goat,
prop her clothesline up.
Then trudge down a path
through Corktown past The Dream,
a mined out Mother Lode,
south of the Mountain Con
above the ridges of the old
abandoned Donkey Road.

The Alice Pit appears,
empty as a starling's song,
her long ladders gone,
a sunken cake of chalcopyrite,
a small acidic lake
above the wounded town.
No trade, selected light,
no tin hat to fit my dome
or pick to hang upon my belt.
Walking west on Waukesha
I am what I perceive,
dancing round the open grave.

A whirl of Peacock's feathers
fell to mark the shaft that finally failed
now flooded green,
the rich rock gone like blood
from a mortal wound,
the cash flow to Phoenix, Arizona.
The solution's in the wind
that plucks my silky beard.

I am amazed. King Kong is dead.
There is no need to vote.

THE MANE OF THE COLD PONY

It is almost yesterday.
Soft flakes drift
lightly by the window,
a past world out there.
No world news
of Japanese economic calamity,
the birth of quintuplets.

I know the pony is cold
hunkered down in the snowy meadow
tail tucked under, dreaming of oats
with cut apples, the girl
with the red hair and pail,
who sometimes comes.

So why do I have the tube on?
Even the small black and white
is out of step with the weather.
The Appaloosa dreams
of a warm barn, head deep
in star crystals, the mist
of his billowy breath.

Paranoid for months
naked and alone all day
in my pad, the answering machine
tangles in its roots
dense as a clutch
of English professors
in an Internet chat room.
I know the gist of the day
could be found simply by walking
over there
with a handful of oats.

Then by combing out the mane

       of the cold pony.

QUICK SILVER RAIN

Growing old, skin slow,
transparent, violet,
thoughts attendant.

Days and Nights of rain.

The loneliness
of country roads,
the dusty reflections
of a vanishing past
down which I peer
in vain.

Days and Nights of rain.

A dance with my shadow
alone, rainwater drops
racing damply downward.
The race on my one and only
window…

Yes, Dragonfly sadness!

BUTTE, NOUVEAU

Townies take vitamins
read poetry
watch the night stars
through telescopes
listen to Jazz
do Yoga,
knowing through epiphany
they could have seen
Shakespeare in The Round.

I think of the bluish green mud
caked on Howard's boots,
the copper sores on Al's leg,
plugged sewers. The chill
of the thirty-eight hundred,
the sound of the cage against
slick skids, the graveyard,
day-night, day-night.

Part of my karma. Still
I do not want to see the Pope
nor do I think I am in touch
with the lives I may
have lived as a Copper King,
nor found in memory, scene
or theatre more dramatic
than my father's lamp and helmet
hanging in the tool shed.

SWEET TOMATOES

There is much to be said

    for false summits

They remind us

    it is a climb

Forepleasure

    is where it is.

The young men don't know

    the joy of no place.

The old men seek

    handholds on the cliff,

in the summer,

    cold sweet tomatoes.

MEMOIR

I have never had dinner on Halloween with a lover,
I often have had Easter dinner with a whore.
Three different women over the years. I remember
fine occasions. Each set a lovely table.
They liked what they did, the girls.

I do not think my sexual claims to experience
stand much chance by comparison, though I had
much in common, including a number of love affairs,
a couple or three of which didn't touch me very deeply.

I knew what they knew. Kisses can be more significant
than couplings. We got together to eat.
Lamb in one instance, salmon in another.
There was wine. I think the people
who scold me for liking to eat should go hungry.

In heaven I will eat with those girls again.
But who I might carve a final pumpkin with remains
a mystery.

BRING ME A COMB FOR MY HAIR

The night my mother died
she said to me on the phone,
"Come down, I am going to have to go
to the hospital."

We visited a while
in her trailer house when I got there.
She was not unhappy,
but in pain.

"Cancer is proof there is no God,"
she said, defying me to argue.
"What will I do?" I asked,
agnostic, middle-aged and insecure,
"If you make a die of it?"
We talked that way, but this time
I made her angry.
Perhaps even bored her.

She said with an odd laugh,
"Maybe it will make a man of you."
Then we sat in silence, until
I knew, though blind,

she could see the tears in my eyes.
She said, sternly then,
"Keep writing," as though
she were speaking to a fool.

On the way to the hospital
she added, "In the morning,
if I am still alive,
bring me a comb for my hair."

OLDE BUTTE RAT

I will not end up like the beggar
with the sign that reads "Need Food," even though,
of course, honesty may be everything.

I think a philosopher should have
      something to talk about,
a writer something to write about.
I have never been able to do more than declare
I am a chip on the foamy river,
and on the chip, "Hey," I say, "I'm still afloat."

Rumi wrote, "Beyond ideas of wrong doing,
beyond ideas of right doing,
there is a field. I'll meet you there."

I wonder who might bring bread? That's what I wonder.
Why a field? "I'll meet ya in the alley," I say.
      Of course, I am
from Butte, not Silky Persia or Smooth Move,
Amerika.

Still. It is the Indian Paint Brush Flowers and Bear Grass
that get to me, as I fork through the sausage
or current affairs, remembering the sacred little mining
operations of the past.

It is also the sky without contrail.
To gaze at the heavens now is to peer through
a shattered windshield,
cracked up by lawless noisy aircraft.

Sometimes I catch a glimpse of blue…

CHILD'S PLAY
(for John Lawry)

She found it
a rock she liked
along the path we walked
or was it John
to whom she tendered it?

After I tossed it
back to the side
where all rocks
were child's play?

I was old   so old
worried about war.
John with children
almost adult
bent down   got the stone.

Tucked it away
in his weathered briefcase   took it
to Europe
with worries
like my own

Where they say
he broke down,
returned though
a year later.

Met us one day
on the same trail
as if by appointment,
to dig out the stone
from his leather case.

To kneel down
and hand it to my daughter
who realized then
why he had come back.

My understanding
grew firmer too.

MIDNIGHT BLUE DONKEYS

Indian summer night bats flicker,
clip the mothy shadows
behind the Power Company's
vapor light.

Cool after the recent rain
two late night beasts,
long hair hanging,
smelling of mountain grass,
reclaim the town.

Midnight blue donkeys
walking . . .

RED TONGUE

I sleep late
Tho early or late
mean little
on Indian time.

I awaken a line
in a poem,
read an hour
take a shower,
wash my face with
kiss my ass soap.

Consider Job,
love and death,
isolation, swimming.
Lifeguards.

All the while
naked in my garret,
alone, thinking
of the shy black dog
with the great red tongue, laughing
by the river.

Listening
        to Stravinsky
                on my radio.

CHEW ON, CHEW ON
(for Bill Bradford)

If there is a God,
because there is a God
we were taught
judgment will be perfect,
but what is thought anyway?

Walking yesterday
along the Sorry River
my friend and I came upon a tree
felled by a beaver,
a big tree, by God.

It fell across
a cement retainer wall,
as though the fall was aimed
by a last resistance
in the toothy beaver's brain.

The beaver is not convinced
his work is inferior
to the Corps of Engineers
the City Fathers hire
to keep the river tame,
not convinced
his dams are less significant.

I love the beaver
and my old friend
who laughed like hell
in appreciation,
figuring the beaver
might hear him, take heart,
and chew on, right or wrong,
by God, chew on.

WIND HORSE RISING
(for Dexter Roberts)

Rain falls,
trees are drenched,
all waving, evergreen
                refreshed.

The moon tho walked upon
remains private.

Messages exchanged.

Hospitals, like prisons,
to be avoided
Mauve corridors,
et al,
schools are bad,
competition over nothing.
Chalk boards squeak,
Halls smell ugly.

There is a breeze
moving through our mutual memory
that chases the bad air away
through the room,
on out the door.

The butterlamps flicker.
Windhorse rising again.

Somewhere a surf breaks upon
a subliminal shore,
interpretation clears:
pictured petroglyphs
come to mind.

A score of tiny old men
killing a blue bear.

The windhorse is rising.

POTATO

A day for a common feast.
By and by, the pomme de la terre.

I awaken in the icy morning,
snow covering the rooftops,
chill creeps into old crevices.
My hands are cold when I wash.
I notice a new liver spot.
As I study the odd map, the territory
above my rusty knuckles.

Face to face with a cold potato.
Friends, far away, distant.
Money short—
Warm in my rented room,
warm enough. Safe for the moment,
probably the remainder
of this day . . .

In spite of the pounding
upon my door last night, a knocking
upon my flimsy door.
"Who's there?" I ask.
A mistake, I figure.
Someone looking for someone
out of the chill of the evening.

Who but the inner folks
in my dreams could know
of my hideout? I mean
here, at the top of the stairs?

I am awakened from a dream
of a dead girlfriend
disappearing as I kiss
her too soft lips. She says,
"You sissy, you."

Just the truth, these lines,
last night, my life,
at the top of the stairs.

The cold potato
heats in the microwave.
I wonder who was in fact,
knocking at my door?

I dice up the clean spud,
sprinkle on the black pepper
and add a pat of butter,

a long time later . . .

BLACK CHERRY SPRITZERS

After we talked with the poet
wearing the etched beard like a drawing
we sojourned by the river and I cried
to hear the ice crack up,
feel the warm air, my tears,
a lull in the winter, and to tell
you small bones, how often I slept there.
Nearly dead by an unknown river!

We leaned in to one another
in the Yuppie Coffee shop,
you in your clever hat, dear Norsky,
not a beret but a double crown.
The wind warm from Iceland, smelling
of lutefisk and steaming butter.

As usual, like dogs we pawed deeply,
whimsically, for whatever lies buried
within, crusty below, the snags
of a lifetime, the bones of contention,
the half stick of gum in your pocket,
the fact that the CIA helped kill
Allende, the reason I say,

"I am Pablo Neruda, Sheryl Noethe."

Today, I'd be lost, if you didn't know,
neither of us needs more nor less
than forever . . .

Thanks for the spritzer.

ALL MY CHANGE

What is it anyway,
the run of time, each step's
success or failure,
at last a foot in the grave,
the final bag of lime?

Games, crimes,
highways, black rain,
the monstrous airplane,
the telephone game.

You might die anywhere
facing a line of broken glass,
overheat, go out with a gasp,
go unread even,
though you hum to prevent
cardiac arrest.

Reaching for a pen, at last,
certain you have something
to say, someone to remember
to repay, a cock for
What's His Name,

a debt . . .

DEEP BELLS

THE OLD POET

A nerve clicked like a switch
in my elbow. I dropped the pick,
waited in the man-way, delicate,
next to rock and timber,
puzzled by the lack of rhythm
the flickering electric,
gumbo on my boots, a dull dynamite
headache.

The round would go with a moan,
a lasting rumble
a slow, low grade, 40% powder
working in red caky rock
we hoped would break easy,
the hanging wall looked shaky.

A day later, her eyes beckoned
as she slipped upstairs
past me, the blind miner,
who sipped black coffee,
muttered about the price
of copper and what was happening
underground in Chile.

DR. BUTTE

They said he had cures for everything
depression even
when the economy was a chance sore
everyone wore along with old hats
out of World War II.

He didn't fake it, they said
he had the medicine
glue with mold, primitive,
older than penicillin,
older perhaps than copper.

As old as bone, better than money,
for which cancer could be stopped
dead in its intricate path
but not radiation or tea,
simple cell glue, like friendship.

But organic not spiritual
put on like honey on toast
with a deep chuckle as if
a wordless benediction.
"There," Dr. Butte said.

We were cured of blight
of dirty sky, of brown buildings,
cured of the late twentieth
century.

Dr. Butte provided the glue
so we could go on
so our fingers would work
and our graves would wait
undug in the green cemetery.

PORTRAIT OF A PHOTOGRAPHER

In the midst of many
at Eddie's Place
in the glass
below opaque foam
the thin man
sees a view
stiff hedge over lip
of his country-rock image,
then tips with care
the joint's cold work of grace
the frosted brew.
In the midst of many
(without haste),
he rolls his own
lets velvet fall
seeks the edge
enjoys the absurd game
above the sinew
above the bone
beyond the taste of beer.
In the midst of many
he kindles a match
eyes alert to laugh
above the flame
to call the shot
to carve the line
to catch in a camera click
a view that contains
us all.

DEEP BELLS

Old turtle, city of my dead youth,
city of tired miners, glory passed
over by Rock Stars,
whose music wails around the Church.

City of Frank Little,
who dying here did not know
how dark it could be elsewhere.

City of deep bells shadow of ancient
buildings beneath which I walked to school,
heard how they crucified Christ
and cried when Bumpo kicked me hard
under the table.

City of the Columbia Gardens,
of Copper Power and Gravel Gertie,
of real ravioli, wine and cheese,
of Tarot packs and plain cards,
five card draw at a mile high,
mystic mountains, blue sky, that
furls around the town, still as hesitant air.

City of Stiff Back Dan, who they said,
read too much when he was young,
stuttered when he spoke and bit
his tongue. This is a place of private
struggle, povitica and pumpernickel,
mortar and cobblestone, union songs,

Arco, booze, and the open pit,
a home of minerals, a place
with an underground to face,

Druidic celebrations, people, flow,
tolerance and patience.
I am initiated and I know.

THE GREEN LEGEND

Legends say green stones
protect a man or woman
from witchcraft, evil spirits, or dark rains
in general; in particular
the charm must be found,
or received as a gift of labor,
chosen from a sluice for luck
or given by a friend,
taken from a heart.

Red stones are rubies,
translucent and cool as poetry,
a gleam in some stream,
a tiny bay in the Clark Fork,
or just down from Gem Mountain,
or any place you believe.

Rocks of every color:
green, orange, lavender, pink,
cast their fire.
Clouds drift white as paper
across the sun-bleached sands
of time.

I ignore my shyness, dry tears,
the dragonfly in the room,
ignore the superstitious hills,
the fact I've known you for years
dial your new number in my dreams
then dredge for precious stones
in Imagination River.

You are lovely in your bones, your brown eyes
enchant the trout,
spellbound in the water,
where as gleeful as a child
I find that green sapphire
you wanted once to see your eyes
absorb protection from.

THE RED CANYON SUITE
(for Joan)

The burnt sienna earth grew cold
beneath our bones,
the white light, a tiny glow,
licking at the edges of the snow.

I loved you then in your brown cords,
the nicest little wrap around,
made it clean curled up,
Iguana on the ground.

I do not think it short term luck
that brought us there,
a good driver, careful in my lap,
the dawn golden in your hair.

Kate was chilled in the silver coach.
I slithered out, leaving copper
in the tent, checked the oil.
That night we paid no rent.

The shapes were gargoyle, pink, red, brown,
the juniper twisted love and hate,
an intricate desert song, the wind
plucked from Flamingo stone.

The sun rose aluminum,
the highway hot and black,
the girl behind the wheel
writing history on macadam slate.

The snaky Interstate
slipped through clay and bluff
past the great horned goat,
sage and scrub cedar the horizon.

I saw a single dancing image,
queens, back to back,
buried in my leather coat.
I smiled to dream and slept.

At every curve my fortune waits,
a graceful pirouette,
a pack of flashing cards,
a deck, a one-eyed jack.

I will play the hand I'm dealt,
have seen a heart straight,
heard the music
of The Red Canyon Suite.

A WREN'S NEST
(for Marylor)

We took an unused road by a leaning pine
that grew despite the efforts of a cat
which years before spilled trees into the draw.
Your talk was something seen,
like an open hand.

I was tired too, that day, full of un-
organized emotion and a sinking will;
the world was new along the creek
and quaking-aspen, the dog chasing the smell
of gophers, dust rimming his black nose.

We walked under a country sky
which cast cloud-shadow on the earth
that turned beneath our feet.
We moved through gates of consequence,
dates of birth and death.

As usual we explored our childishness.
From what still seems a grown-up-point-of-view
you made out connections that led
from stone to stone—the things
we could claim we knew.

The girls, who that morning came home
singing with a catch of trout,
hearts so full that even a fool
could feel the thrill of cool, dark holes,
and beaver dams beneath their eyes.

We combed over common ground,
the events of our lives,
held by a feeling we had endured
to walk that afternoon
close to a wren's nest on a bushy hill.

The four fragile eggs in the nest
were hard to walk away from too, though
we were the intruders. The hen
had stayed until the last safe instant
before she fled, leaving her unborn brood.

We were left to step cautiously away
from the past, and from the peered-at-nest,
to whistle at the dog and start back,
I felt the wonder of being, at that moment,
and then, of heading home.

DREAM INTERROGATIVE

How dare you interrupt my repose,
at such a time as this,
where I hear a quarrel every day?
Your distorted images are intolerable,
even after I awake they do not go
away.

Had I known you better,
been a sly servitor,
I could take my dark temper,
end the argument inside,
regain my poise.

I saw your house,
against the star picked night
lost in mercurial mist.
I stumbled up the stair
breathing still into a void
where no footsteps fall.

I journeyed in your domain
where time does not prevail,
howling along the window sill
outside. I found you behind a door,
then something tapped me
into wakefulness, and a face
behind a face began to laugh,
cracked, became a map
and settled to the floor.

FIFTH CENTURY BUTTE
(We are all the sons and daughters of the mines)

I love this room.
The door has a tiny door in it
designed, wrought of iron filigree,
something the Colombian Fathers
might have found in fifth century Ireland,
the coat-of-arms of a religious warrior.

Who knows when I will see you
standing there? Outside my little door.
The divide is prehistoric death:
Mastodon, elephant, and dinosaur.
Bones erode beneath the snow.

The sky is an ocean. Documents
may be found to prove this.
And the ice-age will melt away
in the warm fiction
behind my little door,
the shafts will be covered,
the pit will become a lake,
and the old miner with the silky
dead hair will return home.

A TIP OF THE HAT

When you are with me
and I ask you if you are happy
and you say honestly
yes
I know I have changed your misery
and you still hate to be happy,
God you hate it.

I have a surprise for you.

Anyone who could write,
". . . songs work their way down . . .
settle in, set up housekeeping,
plan to stay awhile,
creep under my rugs, whistle up from
my teakettle, harmonize with the
jagged purr of my cat, putter
around in my throat and belly all day,
just odd jobs . . ."

can become a finer poet
than Levertov,
better than you know,
my fine-minded friend,
a confident playful spirit.

This is not a poem
in case you didn't notice.
Nor criticism either
but sometimes you simply
struggle to say something

and a break comes even in
a bad poem that is so nice,
so free, so lucky, so starry
that I am knocked a-winding

You are that way.

Have fun with me.
Don't be touchy nor call yourself
lazy nor think at all of rejection slips.

The language is ours.

DUST JACKET

Look
the quiet image, down to earth,
a man from a measured distance.
I'll buy him a drink,
dark Colombian coffee.

What does it matter,
sadness? Many must know it.
Many are alone. Some are alone
and don't know it.
I am alone. I know it.

The bandit on the inside
of the dust jacket proves it.
But that is my brother,
the tired actor
the sad romantic . . .

I met him years ago
walking down a country road
looking for a handout
with those pleading eyes,
saying, saying what?

"Pass the applejack," or
"I'll play Jessie James."
He insists with a wink,
draws his pearl handled colt.

I go on with my poem,
"Be careful, my brother,
I say, raising my hand
with the pen.
"We're both getting older."

NEW POEMS

WINTER RUNOFF

Skimmet's daughter plays the piano,
everyone applauds. The bartender
shakes round dice for drinks.
The juke box is silent
waiting out the final days of winter.

The plank barsill is loaded
with chunks of high grade ore.
Dark galena, peacock copper,
pink mag, ruby silver, even tin
molds along the mirror.

The double decker oil-drum stove
glows with stolen company coal
fed lump by lump with laughter,
sighs of months gone by,
talk of how to turn a dollar.

Men with gnarled and knotted
hands clump arthritic knees,
steam rises from bulky coats
soaking in a pool of heat.
Slush trickles down the eaves.

Those old men against the wall
are smiling once again to hear
select and ancient drain pipes
siphon off the water.

SACAJAWEA
(for Kay)

At moments one would least expect
fate spins her wheel. Once again
everything's unreal. "We don't care
if it rains or freezes, we've got
a statue of the mother of Jesus."
Clouds are puffs of white so pure
cotton would not compare.

My sky today is as empty as a dead
wolf's lair. The night came down
like lead stained with discontent,
doubt, an oceanic menstrual flow,
an old bedspread unraveled
by a cat . . .

The phone, an icy handle, glazed
with sweat. The only light
a burning cigarette.
But isn't this the way it is?
Isn't change so certain, hope
is just a side of despair?
No rock out there, meat,
or metaphor so strong a myth
can begin to mean more than a friend.
Who but fools say faith out loud
in days like these in Butte?

What's make-believe satisfies the most.
The ghost of yesterday's blues fastens
us to thrills. I know this.
Look at the sky, the cute magic
in the air. My necessary angel
climbs a stair, turns, sees me
hunkered there, mere man, stops
blows a lock of hair.

Let's trust the earth that turns
beneath our feet, hate the make-believe,
a world modeled on social myth.
Who insists we dare not see?
Fate spins her wheel and always
visions falter and lose their range.

Experience should be trusted.
I may be late for the final supper.
It takes time, grave art, for love
to heal the heart, to grasp for good,
the true, the real.

MINEYARD BLUES

My sister played a wicked tune.
Her keys were white and black.
Her touch was strong poteen
cached in the shack out back.

My father blew a trumpet
and soon the notes he hit
tilted up the roof top
curved around the moon.

My uncle was a swinger
who morning, noon, and night
floated off in rhythm,
his nose reflecting light.

My mother was a thinker
who read her way to Zen,
figured everything that happened
would probably happen again.

My brother was a talker,
who played a kettle drum,
until they put him in the pen
for running Daddy's rum.

My teacher was a fat man
who sang of hidden streams,
sailed his craft in sadness
into a pool of dreams.

My woman was a vivid person
pleased with a red guitar.
She strummed with tough dark passion
that kept me out of the bar.

Oh, I never missed the action
had a hell of a time in school,
found my fate wasn't fiction,
that I was a God damn fool.

THE HOUSE WRECKER

In the sky
beneath the scaffold where I work
the nearest pigeon
seven stories below
coughs before he dives
through city fog
toward fish markets & butcher shops.
With tools as certain
as these hands
I rip up ledges of big money.

No white Russian or even red
I salute all revolutions
and will survive the ruins.
Trouble taught me what I know.
To scale the heights,
acknowledge cash and religion,
honor hardtack and demolition,
to laugh real laughter,
genuine as bonded goods
stolen from a rich man's cellar.

Far from earnest wars
my managed hammers pound and roar.
Plaster falls from crumbling churches.
Forty bucks an hour makes me smile
to hear you muckers whine
your lack of power—
as I drill down
the glass and mortar castles
of the Empire City.

THE UPPER BUNK

From the high-backed bunk above,
a thin girl urges obedience.
The lively sister awake below
spurns the honored word
and longs for love.

Who is to say which selfishness
best serves the greater wisdom?
One heart prefers to leap
from law to love and touch.

Another wants to make and climb
the rungs to take the upper bunk.

MAIN STREET TABLE CLOTH
(for Jim & Jana)

We danced in the back room
to an old tune by Cheap Cologne,
survived the flooded shafts
that finally failed
as the deep snow fell
like flour from a sifter.
Talk leapt from stone to stone
through the icy winter.
Death and sorrow stood back,
live music shook indifferent air.

Keen on leaky flowers that con
devotion from the bees,
we prospected together
knowing private dreams prevail.
We sought a lost mine
on a dark day in deep timber
and a mountain hot spring
clear as a blue sapphire.

We smiled at one another,
the beekeeper and I,
and at the sure-footed queen
of The Silver Dollar
who tipped a bottle to pour
white wine in a fine glass
with an odd laugh
out of the sixteenth century.

Like a clean table cloth,
milk, honey, and fresh bread,
love whispers suddenly
of things ahead.
Beyond the brick wall,
beyond the fluctuating price
of peacock copper,
the moon is universal coin.

We will think of you walking
along a sandy beach,
or around a campfire supper,
waving to the whales
or standing in a field of clover,
love you both, no matter,
and whatever.

THE OLD JAZZ POET

He ambled through the room
scattering lamps and tables
dragging from his pocket
the crumpled sheets of paper
saying "It's pretty good.
I tell you. It's really there."

Looking at the paper
cut into the whiteness
we saw only his black blood
the pride of his ink.

Cigarette smoke burned
our eyes as we humored him
through the long night.

In the morning dawn
we left him stretched
on his davenport
a body on marble
breathing from a far away place.

In the evening he awakened
and his laser beam eyes
smoked holes in the shade.
He lifted his horn
made a sound like a Ram's
cooler than Jesus
richer than sex.

After a while
he dug out the poems
laughed whole notes
as he sat
on his ceramic throne
dreaming of real things.

THE ESCAPE

The jungle has cleared in his eye.
The man has a plate in his brain.
The price of the medal was high.
Fat Annie is dancing again.

(sing slowly)
      Cor
          re
             gi
                dor.

      Cor
          re
             gi
                dor.

Walls move in the prison.
There's a death march to Bataan.
There is no booze in heaven.
Fat Annie swings the con.

Medics will nurse the liver.
Braille will touch the blind.
Fat Annie will lift the silver
From the pocket of his mind.

No one holds a chain or gun.
Ghost guards leave the door.
Skulls grin smooth in the sun.
Fat Annie shakes the floor.

(sing slowly)
    Cor
        re
           gi
              dor.

    Cor
        re
           gi
              dor.

The juke box plays "Corregidor."
His bones will make a scene.
The dead will dance once more
in the bedroom of a queen.

CALL FOR A CAB

His taxi,
its long checkered hood
concealing the low black engine,
a row of pistons pumping,
the slight click of a tappet
signaling . . .

The dealer in tatterdemalion,
tapping the cards up his sleeve,
his ignition system
idle and purring
waiting for a fare—a kinetic sedan.

"Get in my Silver Cloud," he said,
shuffling an incredible deck,
prowling the thoroughfares,
alive with new leaves
of a real Garden City.

Arm in arm with his passengers,
he pulled away from the curb
the fame and the sun
which he hoped would not set
upon him, the taxi, our city, me,

or the sudden significant spring.

THE WEB AND STAR

Shy and ubiquitous
in the mine underground
a canary in a coal chute
a white mouse in a Copper set
the lagging loose and full
the headboards bulging.

He is hanging on
as the spider on my hand
turns about to see the silk
is gone. He knows a strand
remains as He brushes off
His hand. A filament floats

through the sunlight, a wisp
of web caught by a star.
A gossamer remains . . .
My eyes track the drift
sliding into the Invisible
Thought of home where the dark
lives in the light . . .

Everything teeters
in the thin air and balances
my tea cup on my knee
as She plays jump rope
one, two, three . . . and asks

Do you believe in God, Grampa?

JOKERS WILD

The name of the casino where the hound
to Butte stops now where disabled travelers
in search of crossroads and transfer
totter about with tickets to somewhere.

He got off the red eye remembering
the last far away thing she said to him as he
walked from the house, his bag packed.
"Taking baths always made you funny."

There is an Indian man in the casino
who speaks of his wyf as though
he had read Chaucer.
There is a big relief as is the chief,
an old Salish warrior
with black walnut eyes
and a nose big enough to ride home on.

"For any wannabe and a cup of coffee,"
he mused and he hated her always
and his smile curved like a bow,
that at the end of his final ride
even the mortician took note of. . . .

SMALL SACRIFICE

I just burned up a pan on the stove,
the smoke finally thick enough to impress me.
An omen, I figure, a little warning, a reminder
that I have miles to go before I succumb, by God!

A Laotian woman just stuck her head in my doorway,
open to free the trapped smoke billowing,
to check on me, a big toothy smile, as if to say,
"You burn food too, eh?"

"Not to worry," I tell her, smiling back, as
if my dinner was a sacrifice to the third world.

COOL AS A NINE MILE WOLF
(for Roger)

A pond with fish.
I walk among the fish
in the cool water
that rises from springs
at its bottom.

It helps me,
gives me a balance,
the sun I need.
Something simple,
just there, a dragonfly
with blue indigo wings.

I have thoughts
there that I could not
understand, if I
stayed sequestered
in the town cocoon.

Eighteen miles or so
in my tapacata queep
on the frontage road,
fast enough for me,
dangerous even.

I go there alone too.
For some reason wandering,
getting old now.

Looking for a home,
peering into the water,
the deep mirror of water.

White river rock,
deep green moss,
Sun fish, Rainbow trout,
ancient red sand,

K-Mart kids wading,
swimming.
At night, campfires
Song dogs . . .

A CUT OF LIGHT

Chilled by diamond drills
in the mine, concerned over
burned bridges, I rip up gutted
poems, learn to cruise,
a pterodactyl cracked out
of nature's glacial design.

With the eyes of a cave-born
reptile I scan the drift
for the giveaway sign
of my shadow escaping
the rib-timbered flesh
of the mountain of words,
the bone of the muse.

Gunning the engine,
I move past the heart
into the cut of light.
Moth-hungry for flame,
the shape of the carbon,
I seek the vein,
mother lode,
of a craft-ridden art.

OPEN SPACES

Shadows of the water skippers,
dune buggies on the creek bottom,
race where I ride the open space.
When she sees what I see I feel
a soft lovely thrill stir the leaves,
where I peer shyly from the Elm trees,
and the fat-assed owl pussies whoo,
night eyes as big as silver dollars.

In a moment I hear a trout tail slap
the muddy river as if to say aloud
in a new way a new word, a new sound,
and then it is so quiet, so still,
I see inside the shadows a design,
the river pouring water toward the seas,
and the fat-assed owl pussies whoo.

Water, water, river rock and otter,
Osprey feathers in the wind and me,
the fat guy, Grandfather Ed,
tickled pink and gleeful,
just a trifle blue, grins around
the edges of the sky, dreams
of a honeymoon of graces
where no one ever has to die.

CALL TO ARMS
(for Jenny Warwick)

The electric chill
scrapes deserted streets
of the one o'clock city.
Beyond reason I cross
the mountain pass.

I come for her body.
The wind eddies in the corner
of my eyes.
I march to her parlor.

The skirts of the town
sing choice choir notes.
Her voice whispers
a chime like the "come"
of my woman.

She is cold on the slab
and solemn. So solemn
she says, "I love you."
Her body, naked
and warm in my blood.

GRANDMOTHER

When I walk in she is surprised
and says, "My, but you look so grown up."
She gives me a huge slice of mince pie
and her eyes dance and she laughs
and she slaps her thigh and everything
is the same as it was a lifetime
earlier in the warmth of her kitchen.

Autumn snow outside the farmhouse
falls like flour from a sifter
covering the tracks back to cities,
apartment house, offices, burned bridges,
talk, fear, the chill of ambition
and the hope that my art can compete
with the warmth of her kitchen.

APGAR AND AFTER
(for James Dorr Johnson)

Wind-blown waves break
Pearl white over your grey hair
At Flathead Lake
beneath the chilly sun
at the bay the ducks claimed
where the dog
with the hurt eyes
the barman hates
fights the rope,
tied on the misty shore
of the whipping lake.

North and later
the salmon at Apgar Bridge in Essex
feed themselves as fated sacrifice
to Eagles down from the mountains.
keen in grateful talons,
A roily feast free of unrequited love,
untouched by neglect,
or the spider web of sentiment—
the Kokanee at least are free.

I recall for no reason
her laughter in bed
as rich as whiskey cake,
the grave intimacy of a thigh,
insistent as a rolling salmon
the scales and feathers of a love affair,
two dozen saxophones
a hundred geese nattering overhead,
a ticker tape of grey
for us old friend.

At the Essex Railhead,
A locomotive purrs and whispers.
Downstairs the boy barman longs
for the bright lights of Big Sandy,
ignores the birds
nesting in the tamarack
a thousand yards away.

Mindful of the final cycle
I watch the eagles reel in the mirror,
West of the Shy Fellows,
East of the Blue Missions
where gold and silver have no say
as we slip through silky
forest green down
the black new highway
toward another day.

AFTER THE COPPER MINES FAILED

The Company pulled out
to write The Hill operation off
as a tax loss,
and city fathers spoke
of sentimental history
instead of evil.

Local artists were commissioned
to portray Western Scenes
on the east wall
of the Miners' Bank,
calculated to convey
the hard rock glories of yesterday.

It was thought by some
avaricious history
might keep us together,
like the memory
of a succulent supper,
until the town's buildings began
to burn, one by one,
like candles on a cake.

Stores and shops shut their doors,
houses were deserted
leaving curtainless windows
to stare at tourists
who strolled the streets
like actors on
a vacant movie set.

Wives who hated "hell holes"
grew morbid without a monthly check,
seldom combed their hair
or smiled men male, and left
neglected children to lurk about
black-iron gallows frames,
smoking cigarettes.

Miners who did not wander off
to Idaho, nursing hopes of silver,
drank too much, grew mean in bars,
muttering to one another
of explosive rounds that would go
with a sexual shudder,
leaving bornite like broken dreams
on the floors of flooded stopes.

A critic wrote that I was
"Just a small town Marxist . . ."
"Sure," I said, "but quite friendly,
merely curious about The Company,
and what happened to the Indians
in Chile,
after the C.I.A. murdered Allende."

LEAVING THE POOL

"She handed me a blue teddy bear
then headed for Cody, Wyoming."

A riff of music shivers in the open air,
a cultural boombox in the distance
and the memory of orange.

Not the orange of Northern Ireland,
a longing for silence, the sweet orange,
puritan truth, Plymouth Rock, coarse horse hair

a pure white trillium, wondering if here
is home, in this wild place, or where?
A hop, skip and jump to homelessness.
Isn't friendship central?

Sitting later in a rocking chair
before a blinking amber light, not quite orange,
the big hand sweeps away the trouble,
trembles in the mind, the tick
explains away the time. I meditate:

No eternal snapshot, but a casket
for Quasimodo's dreams, or better still
in the forest grove by the sacred pool
a still quiet place we loved

to be together in geothermal water,
a grey cement box for Pandora's fears.

A BLUE SAUCER

It has been cold, and I
have been ill,
forced at the same time
to pull my own tooth.

Of course, I seek
another day.

I had the urge
while out walking
to rescue a torn orange
open to the sun
lying in the snow,

to take it in
wash it in cool water
keep it on a blue saucer.

I know the sad side of the street
to look for the value
the taste of true winter.

KATE AND I

Two on the swing at once
one in mind the other swinging just as high
as her mother sits at the wooden table
saying, "Hang on." I push the swing
as carefully as care. My balance I check
with every nerve.

My memory is dark with fear someone dear
might fall but I'm with her and take my turn
at sixty-three. She waves her little finger,
a tree beyond shakes out a leaf in the light.

Her mother says, "Hang on." I slow the swing
my hands around her trim body. God she's small.
We are here because of love. No one seems to know
just why yet we are more than one
and she and I are having fun.

It is sometimes hard to go on in
time is ticking and what can I say?
I held her mother just so and tenderly
pushed her too, up into the sky
where years later she rolled her bug
on a dark night road.

Seven times it turned like a tomato can.
The window snapped off her hair
on the driver's side. It is she
who says, "Hang on."
She's right there. Her star
looks like a rolling tomato can
a shower of meteorites like
rich auburn hair.

A sparkle falling
falling from somewhere like grains
of golden sand where a swinger
draws back a swing up into the sky
and says, "Hang on."

"These babes know how," I say.
The doctor looks away, since he
has a crowded day and knows I can't
stay long for a chat, that I
must be getting back
to her little finger . . .

GRANDDAUGHTER COUNTRY

A caterpillar sits upon my desk.
It has a heart-shaped mouth and
crawls from its cocoon to find
and be a part of beauty.

What is best in the treasure state
requires a will to survive,
a good dog to pull you straight,
the best fate for a mountain girl:
real camping trips to sacred places,
Looking Glass or Chief Joseph.

Anywhere your tent is welcome.
That is my Montana.
Anywhere your tent is welcome.

BIRDS OF A FEATHER
(for Marylor)

A woman I love, my ex-wife
with our infant granddaughter
rounded an aisle
in the new Safeway
where we were shopping.

"There's a sparrow flying overhead,"

she said, when she saw me.
We both looked upwards.
I wanted so badly
to tell her something
she could cherish, so she
would know

that I love her, like her even,
more than I hate her, but all
I could think of was a bird
I once saw shredded
by an exhaust fan.

Feathers floating willy nilly.

She looked so fey
upon hearing my story, shyly,
so shyly, walking away,
pushing the stroller down
another aisle.

Leaving me again, again,
dead feathers gathering
about my feet.

A NOTE FROM THE THIRD WORLD

The Berkeley Pit is filling
even as I stand here,
twenty billion gallons and rising.
I wait for the town I came from
to die inside, for Mozart to be reborn,
to shake hands with Beethoven
and come out joking.

"Our Lady of the Rockies" watches
over the Continental Divide.
Hail Mary. A great name, Mary.
But what's in a name?
Two millennia and the Kingdom of Heaven
seems as elusive as a Buddhist koan.
Simple peace would do.

Something besides working
for the Yankee Dollar, both mother
and daughter, and the Indian woman,
who borrowed five bucks from me
last night on Halloween.

I carved a pumpkin and handed
out the longest night of the year
cookies and coins and gave
a granddaughter a silver salt cellar
for truly we are as Gandhi knew
the salt of the earth . . .

RACK 'EM UP

Locked in chains of damaged nerve
recalling periodic times of hope,
I looked straight into the face of rock.
My drill ready, Big Bertha outside
bellowing, the diesel running low.

I eased the Swede up on its leg
pulled the drill latch and listened to it
churn, the water running down from the center
steel. Four hundred feet underground,
ten feet into a low grade face,
nothing but stamina to urge me on.

Snow billowing past the portal set,
the Ingersol waiting for fuel
to rotate my steel a few more minutes.
In that underground tunnel,
twelve to fourteen rounds to drill
and I'd be through for the shift.

Bang, the drill sticks and steams,
my shoulder aches.

Now, I just look back upon such cold days
as too tough to finish. I discovered myself
and went home early alone and none of it
made a damn bit of difference
except to teach me we have nothing
or damned little to say.
Lee Nye would wave a chalked stick,
"The angle of incidence equals the angle
of reflection," he'd say, and run the table,
search for his gum and laugh.

NO PICK OR SHOVEL

I've been writing notes and letters
sending them to anyone I think
might be a friend. I could sail
them on The Clark Fork River.

I look for myself in the trees,
remember the woods and wilderness.
I see myself high in a gallus frame
close to a shiv wheel
that doesn't turn. Brakes locked.
I am closed down. No ore.

I have a ghost town inside,
vibrant memories of a life.
My friends know the ghosts take care
of me. I am lost in the Garden City.
I made a pass at an Elm tree

as though she might give me her hand
and greenly we'd go. When I am lost
in Butte, I forgive Garrison Keillor
for calling the town
"The Richest Hill on Earth."

I was born there. Mining exhausts
a town. The rich take the riches.
The poor are left with "The Hill."
Barren granite, empty as a rock bee's nest,
a dead stone honeycomb.

I wander around downtown Missoula
Perhaps it is the old miner I see
trudging along beside me in shop windows,
the one with the dead silky hair
who has no pick or shovel.

FOLK TALE

My mother told me
I was born backwards in the early morning.
She told me more but I have forgotten
whether it was early Tuesday or Wednesday
on that July eighth in 1936,
fireworks going off. WWII stirring.

My daughter, a nurse, said I probably
shouldn't make too much of the symbolism,
I might have been born butt first
not feet first and running.

I know it was a theatrical appearance.
My mother had only the day before
waded the Jefferson River in hip boots
and I had got turned around.

It has been that way ever since.
Today I walked five miles to buy
an alarm clock so I won't have to wake up
tomorrow . . .

I am supposed to take a pill
to make me sleep,
but I must wake up to take another pill
so I won't be depressed over insomnia.

Beethoven is a blessing.
Ludwig would have understood why
I walked so far for an alarm clock
so I could sleep. I needed the walk.
I will sleep tonight knowing
I will awake in the morning before
the alarm clock.

THE CABIN

The cabin was simply built
with walls hewn straight
to fit the door. The roof
sags now—arched by time—
no longer squared,
as when I crawled
upon the floor in small
and simple patterns.

Now the walls meet
to slip to ground and form
a smooth organic blur,
no longer sharp,
but crumbling round
the foundations where
distinctions don't occur.

In the soil, or rather sand
sifting through the door
no longer according to man-made
plan, a new shape attempts
erasing sores—
bans memory of order and simplicity
to create a longing for blocks—

something other than the feeling
of an object's mystery.

INSIDE HER

"I'm in deep trouble,"
she said to him,
the first time in history
anyone had spoken of me.

The year 1936, Butte, Montana,
not far from here.
She was 18. He had
just come down the hill,
a shift in the Neversweat,
$2 a day on a widowmaker.

She bawled, then soft tears.
"What should we do?"
"This is a fine time to ask," he said
looking at his muddy brogans,
his face coal dark.

They fought and screamed
at one another, then a long
silence and she asked again, "Well?"
All the while I lay curled up
my heart beating in the darkness
inside her.

ROAD KILL
(for Malcolm)

When finished with the fowl
it is significant how the bones look
on the plate.

I have a friend who is living
on road kill. He told me that a deer
that was run squarely over

is better to pick up
than one tossed into the barrow pit,
its legs akimbo.

I prefer chicken to venison
so every time I eat a bird
I put the bones in order.

I think of my friend prowling
the gutters of the highway
like a hungry vulture.

He walks in his sad boots
down the black asphalt
in search of supper.

Every time I clean a bone
or tidy up a porcelain plate
I think of him.

A SLICE OF WATERMELON

She said, "I'm so nervous
I can't hardly manage. I feel
like punching the wall."

When he hung up he thought
he should catch a plane and go.
She was the only mother he'd know.

A new millennium child of impulse,
the next day he went to the airport
and climbed on board a 747.

When he got there he found her
inside the house, distraught
her hair a tangle of misery.

He put his arms around her
and she stamped her foot and cried
and dug her fingers into his back.

He tightened his squeeze and after
a gasp she began to breathe normally.
He realized they hadn't hugged

in over twenty years. Their life
was a long frustrating telephone
conversation . . .

When he got back from New Jersey,
the phone rang and it was her.
She sounded happy and said,

I have been slicing watermelon
wishing you were still here."
He said nothing, knew he was home.

PAPER LANTERNS
(for Kristy Hager)

There are two senses only: right and left
and what is poured between them. Mindful hands
that are kept open in a dream of cupping.
One attentive to its touching, one that trembles
with the details of amnesia. What you remember
about paper sacks is the way the cold is spelled
across the top, the letters wet and brown.
You learned the word, the depth obsessive other
word for empty and lit up the world
with an imaginary candle that won't blow out
in the night winds of winter.

A specific silence, the surface as orange as moonlight,
all you could pour between two senses. It runs
into many words. Imagine swans
who come to water, how they bring their swimming
with them. The surface is eventful with reflections,
while the orange feet beneath it send
entire landscapes shoreward in lazy circles.
The whirl implies a shore by repetition,
one wave passing into the same hand over, an arrival,
the woman painter, looked at calmly:
sky, a left-hand wind that blows against the right
making motion among the trees across the water
where the shells recline, one cupped out, the other in,
free of the cold we call the wind.

A WALK WITH ROBERT BLY

I slipped out after him,
ran down the dark tree lined
sidewalk to catch up
"May I walk with you?" I asked
as we approached the University Oval.
The poet didn't break stride.
"If you want," he answered
as we walked along.

Ten minutes before we had been
at a party at Dick Hugo's home,
a party given in honor of this man,
who had chosen to read protest poems.
The Vietnam War raged around us
even though on TV it was confined
to the brutalized country of its origin.

"He hates war too," I said,
defending my mentor, Dick Hugo, whose jazz
records he had shattered against a wall
before fleeing into the dark evening
with me close on his heels.
"He just doesn't like protest poems,"
I went on, "thinks poetry should be
personal and private."

"If he doesn't like my poems,
he doesn't like me," Robert Bly replied,
as he picked up his stride as we began
our walk around the oval
on the little campus by the river.
"Now he has something to take personally,"
he said with an odd warlike laugh.

Later that night at home I remembered
the party, the drinking, the argument,
the precious cracked jazz records,
and the aphorism "When the elephants
fight, the grass gets trampled."
I was a young writer and wondered
what I had let myself in for.

LOVE ADMITTED, SLEEP DESCENDED

Don't leave, abandon me,
blow windily
above the shack,
and chipmunk chatter,
the sweep of hawk shadow.
Just don't.

I know enough to stand alone
letting the snowflakes
brand me with their individual
shapes, tender moist mouths,
white as death every winter,
mother.

There is bread upon the table,
a wedge of cheese, a sharp knife
that would fit nicely
in my throat,
dark red blood flowing,
warmly sentimental.

Led away to the cemetery
to a secret grave
from which no whisper
unimagined comes
from the heart-stained soil
beneath the plain stone.

Tonight I curl up
beneath an honest dirty quilt
in your bed, I make myself,
after the wedge of brie
and bread have ended
the sharp knife's lies.

Tomorrow I will sign my name
tend the dead due honor,
kick the snow clumps
off the car, shake hands,
play any game rife
with inner dream.

Love admitted, sleep.

HOT SPRINGS

"Hang there until you can hang no longer,"
the Nez Perce Indian said to me that summer.
"Then drop to the ground and try to sleep."

Earlier in the Cowboy Bar I had told him,
"Charlie, I can't sleep. I keep thinking of the war."
That's when he told me to hang from the tree limb.

The tree with the great limb was at the Hot Springs
just above the little town where I was staying
that summer on vacation from the University.

I felt like a cracked pot, a ceramic mistake.
The potter's wheel had wobbled
leaving me a shapeless lump of clay,

A plug without will or purpose so I did
as Charlie bid, I walked to the Springs.
I found the great willow tree,

I jumped for the limb and hung on
for dear life until my arms ached,
then I dropped to the grass and dozed.

Five precious minutes and my life was renewed
and I knew I could go home and write this poem.
I vowed I would continue my writing practice

until all war ended or I died.

LEAVING TOWN

It was a lonely walk through
the ghost town to the bus depot
where the Greyhounds rested
in a customary line.

My suitcase was made of cardboard,
the snap was broken. It wanted to open.
I clutched it to my hip.

I met her on East Mercury Street.
Noticing my baggage, she said,
"You must be going somewhere."

"I'm leaving town," I said.
"On my way to catch a bus."
"Oh, I'm sorry," she said.

"Nothing to be sorry about,"
I smiled, knowing there are no second
chances for first impressions.

"Have you lived here long?"
"Long enough to know I have to leave,"
I answered whimsically.

"I've seen you before," she said.
"You are a writer, aren't you?"
"I try," I said, smiling again.

"What does writing mean for you?"
"It's what I do," I said. "I sit
at the typewriter and bleed words."

"A bloody writer," she laughed
and took one of my suitcases
as we walked on toward the depot.

I never learned her name but
she hugged me before I got on the hound
and I wished I could have told her

I'd be back.

SPARROW MEDITATION
(for Jack Waller)

A sparrow zooms around the monastery
beating its wings against the window.
Brother Jacque, the atheist in residence,
climbs upon a chair and feels for it.
The bird flies in circles about the room
returns to flutter against the pane
as though in contact with hard air
that traps it and will not separate,
or give before the push of a racing heart.

Watching from his chair the stranger says,
"You have to be quick as a cat."
"Oh," he exclaims, then
deliberately reaches to place one hand
below the wild bird, another over it,
cradling the sparrow for a moment
only to release it out an open window
where it whirrs away in daylight
over brother Lewis's yellow roses
a visual riff of music . . .

Leaving us alone and free
of wild activity and flight.

FORLORN ALLEY

Two nights in the slammer,
now a cold walk down Courthouse alley
behind Murphy's Hotel,
as the County Jail in Butte is known,
in search of what?
"A place to lie my head," he thought,
"a room of my own, shelter."
He could put the touch on Bingo
who ran the flophouse next to The Fox.

He wanted out of the winter,
clear of the long black alley.
He worried about Nam and napalm,
figured brandy was a heart stimulant.
The wind was picking up.
He felt his face with cold fingertips.
He imagined his body stumbling;
the forlorn have no secrets.

Once upon a time
he had owned a house,
of grey stone and red brick,
a two story with nine rooms and many closets,
was married to a woman with brown eyes,
as mysterious as the walk
he was on now, though time
was the critical factor then,
she was twenty years younger than him,
and time was the critical factor now,
it was below zero and growing darker.

WAR GRAY ABSENCE OF SKY

Too many deadlines.
Paydirt is lost
in incalculable cost.

Episodes sing
through the mind. Images
cling to small trees.

A slender Afghan girl
with large green eyes
leans against a wall.

Shriven apples
dangle like baubles,
nuggets of gold.

The twin towers shudder.
The cycles of revenge begin
like pebbles in a pool.

Similes of paradise,
the mold of old myth,
a brassy spittoon.

Into which one could piss
if erection did not require
all of this.

STEEL BRACELETS

Sometimes the bear gets you,
sometimes you get the bear.

You do not kill if you have a sense of humor.
My girlfriend is in handcuffs.
She always taunted cops.
My suitcase is made of cardboard.
My shoes are Irish brogans.

A veteran hired to kill
retires to join the peaceful,
and write books about the battles
he survived because he squeezed the trigger
believing war was natural.

In medieval times in England
there was a word that meant a man
had a knowledge of good and evil
in his heart, an inborn knowledge.
It was not conscience, a Christian concept,
it was inwit.

Earth is something God put together
on one of his bad days, since he allowed people
to go to war and kill one another.
It is a matter of choice. You can chose
good over evil if you have inwit
or you can chose the reverse.

I confess I have not always chosen good,
but I have always refused the call to arms,
always stayed clear of the military,
opposed war as managed murder.

To kill is evil.
I have spent time in jail over these matters.

ALDEN NOWLAN MY FRIEND

I feel guilty
about stealing your poem
but is was by auspicious coincidence,
since I love the poem,
an elaborate accident.

Fifteen years ago or so
I read the poem "It's Good To Be Here,"
and liked it so much
that I scribbled down the lines

I most appreciated on a paper
which got placed accidentally in a file
I called unfinished poems.
God knows why.

Last year I moved across town, papers
were shuffled about on the floor
of my den where I read the lines,
and got pleasantly side tracked.

I hate the work of moving
and reading the scribbled lines
on the floor made me want to finish
something I had started years before.

I could see it had the makings.
I do not think I saved
your lines for later theft,
because I was so surprised to read
my poem in an anthology today

with your name attached.

I must have written them
down as an act of honoring them.
Now I have published them as my own,
and you have gone and died.
It may be too late to apologize.

I am so sorry.

THE MAN NEXT DOOR

It was great what Maggie would do.
She would fly down and land on Penny.
The Cocker Spaniel not to be outdone
would walk about in the yard
with the Magpie on her back.

It was wonderful to see,
as though the dog and the bird
were creating a little act just for me
while I sat inside and watched
through the big window.

Not so wonderful to see was
my neighbor one summer afternoon
shoot Maggie with a shotgun.
The bird had been sitting on his wife's
clothes' line minding her own business.

I think Penny missed her friend
since she walked around the yard
looking upward all the time.
I still miss my winged friend.

I was sixteen and for fifty years
I have hated the man next door.

THE LONG DARK YARD

It was an academic party
where guests stood around with drinks
talking of Milton, Shakespeare,
quoting critics and literary theorists.

The Vietnam War was on however,
and people drank heavily as if there would be
no tomorrow or going home that night.
Men's wives were flirtatious.

A little after midnight I saw her
grimly walk out the back door
onto the deck, take off her ring
and hurl it into the yard.

I saw him then, my friend, standing
between an American Studies scholar
and a Shakespearean looking blank
like God must have looked

when He gazed at Chaos with nothing
on His mind but Himself. It had been
my friend's wife who had grimly
hurled her wedding ring from the deck.

He had watched his wife throw away
their marriage on a fierce impulse
and now he stood becalmed,
his eyes as big as a startled baby's.

It takes two to make a world.
Who knows what to do
when the world stops at the end
of a long dark yard?

INSIDE THE VIRGIN'S HEAD

Sixty ton and ninety feet tall
Our Lady of the Rockies overlooks
Butte, Montana. Some say a lost
town without the memorial statue.

While under construction on
The Continental Divide a steel worker
Inside the Virgin's Head
grabs a megaphone and insists
that everyone get down to the floor.

"Listen up," he says. "I have something
to say to you all." The men join him.
"I have been a mean bastard. Last night
I got drunk and beat up my wife."
He lowers the bull horn, shaken by tears.

The men do not know what to do.
They mill around but are silent
waiting to see if he would go on
They did not know what to do.
No one spoke. Some light cigarettes.

"She is going to leave me," he said,
"unless I get the Virgin's help. That's
my idea, anyway. A miracle."
Men shuffle uncomfortably but
his platform is awesome.

For a true confession no alcoholic could
have chosen a more dramatic place
than the head of the Virgin and though
the men are hardened workers they
remain respectful.

Finally he lifts the bull horn and says
in a shaky tearful voice, "Pray with me,
will you guys, then I'm going home and
I hope to God my wife will be there."
The men bow their heads in prayer.

Afterwards a man yells, "Hang in there pard."
"She'll come around," another adds.
I do not know whether the man's wife
took him back or whether he quit drinking
but I believe in miracles.

CARDBOARD SUITCASE

I headed for the station
It was time to leave.
I had worn out my welcome.
For me the town was dead.
I packed my cardboard suitcase.

Butte was over.
The miners had all died out.
What was left did not suit me,
but I knew it would not end.

Frank Little's memory would
hang on like death. I would
never be anywhere but from there.
A town to toast.

In my memory,
Butte was a mythic place,
where forty-eight head frames
were pulling ore from shafts,
shive wheels turning in the sun.

The bus was right on time.
The driver took my ticket.
I was on my way to Missoula,
the Garden City, home of Big Pink,
the University of Montana.

A new life, a place free of crumbling
brick and mortar. Green lawns,
the Clark Fork River.
"Live by water," my mother said,
"Sleep by a river."

ABOUT THE AUTHOR

Ed Lahey was born in Butte, Montana in 1936. Like his father's, Ed's life would revolve around mining, not only in the hard rock shafts thousands of feet beneath the city itself, but in the many smaller wildcat operations scattered across the western part of the state.

Few if any trades were as physically stressful or potentially fatal as mining back in the day, and this fact no doubt accounts for the fierce sense of pride the miners so openly displayed, Ed Lahey among them. The suits and ties have their stock certificates; Ed had his father's headlamp.

But there was something else brewing inside Ed, something as removed from blasting rock as gardening. Ed was driven to write poetry. All men must seek the approval of their fathers, whether that figure is a kind, tolerant, supportive person, an absentee, or a tyrant. Ed's father seems to have belonged to the first category because when he saw Ed writing a poem at the age of fifteen, he asked to see it, read it, then folded it up and put it in his wallet where he carried it until his death, in the process letting his son know, admittedly in a rather left-handed way, that things would be alright even if he didn't choose to become a lawyer.

Ed went to the University of Montana where he graduated with a degree in English, and a Woodrow Wilson Scholarship, which enabled him to attend the

University of Minnesota for a year. Then it was back to the mines, until learning that Richard Hugo had arrived in Missoula to teach. So Ed went there to study with him, a time he considers critically important to his own development.

Following that, he taught at the University for several years, during which he married, and the couple had two daughters. This however, was a time of unrest and emotional distress. The Vietnam war was at the highest pitch of its violent folly, and Ed, along with so many others, became deeply involved in the growing protests against it. Along with this there was the civil rights movement, so there was plenty to be angry about, and those like Ed, whose voices shouted the loudest, usually did some jail time.

Like so many artists before him, the pressures and expectations of polite, conventional society drove Ed to retreat with his family to an old mining claim far back in the mountains, a place of sanctuary, but without the simplest amenities of running water or electricity. What he learned from that experience is that all the annoying expectations of social conformity were more than replaced by what it took just to stay alive.

When the Idyll ends, as it always does, the forced return to civilization usually results in anger and chaos, and in Ed's case these took the form of depression and divorce. And so it was back to Butte and the mines, which finally was home.

Ed Lahey has received The First Book Award from the Montana Arts Council, and a National Endowment for the Arts writing fellowship. He has been included in a number of anthologies, including *The Last Best Place*. However, as is the case with so many genuine artists who have no interest in, or patience with any part of the bourgeois establishment, a list of its few accolades is absolutely meaningless. What does matter is relentless and honest perseverance, exemplified by forty years of writing and reading throughout the Northwest, guided by the unshakable conviction that Art is the Principle.

A NOTE ABOUT THE DESIGN

When designing a book, our intentions are to enhance and dignify the text, no matter what its style, form or content. This is hardly science by the way, requiring as it does more intuition and feeling than anything else. It's the same old story, which is the search for truth and beauty, in a world where that axiom seems to mean anything from pure white to coal black.

The most beautiful frame in the world can do nothing to improve the quality of a painting, anymore than an exquisitely constructed book can make the writing better. However, in the case at hand, the writing is as beautiful as it gets, and after all, it must live somewhere, so why not make it as right as can be? You can't look at a painting without also seeing the frame, and you can't read a book without holding it in your hands.

Visually speaking, there is much to be dismayed about on bookstore shelves these days, essentially a nearly complete capitulation to commerce as dictated by persons with master's degrees in business administration. Is it being blindly sentimental to say it wasn't always like this? When you pick up a copy of Ernest Hemingway's *Green Hills of Africa*, published by Charles Scribner's Sons in 1935, what strikes you foremost is that it is appropriately plain, and above all has the simple look and feel of the prose itself. Is it beautiful? Well, strictly speaking, no not really. But it's not ugly or thoughtless, or insulting either, and by a simple process of elimination, achieves, if not true beauty, a most acceptable charm, which feels just right.

We tend to like our books to be a bit larger than today's convention would have it. This costs a little more, but it contributes to what we hope is a generous attitude, and we go out of our way to make sure the tail never wags the dog. The same thing applies to the paper, boards, cloth and stitching. In choosing and sizing the type for this collection, we set headlines and stanzas in about a dozen fonts, all of classic, time tested design, then spent hours, days, weeks, staring at comparisons, with as blank a mind as possible, until the visceral visual message eliminated one, then another, and another, the choice finally stating itself, in this case the typeface called Garamond.

```
Book Shelves
 PS3562.A33 B57 2005
Lahey, Ed
Birds of a feather : the
complete poems of Ed Lahey
```

DATE DUE

Demco, Inc. 38-293

CANISIUS COLLEGE LIBRARY
BUFFALO, NY